Viola

STRINGS FOR ALL. Pops

Solos-Duets-Trios-Quartets
For Any Combination of String Instruments
Optional Piano Accompaniment

Arranged by Michael Story

© 2010 Alfred Music Publishing Co., Inc.
All rights reserved. Printed in USA.

ISBN-10: 0-7390-7633-7
ISBN-13: 978-0-7390-7633-0

ANY WAY YOU WANT IT

VIOLA

Words and Music by
NEAL SCHON and STEVE PERRY
Arranged by MICHAEL STORY

37027

OVER THE RAINBOW

Music by
HAROLD ARLEN
Arranged by MICHAEL STORY

37027

BOULEVARD OF BROKEN DREAMS

Words by BILLIE JOE
Music by GREEN DAY
Arranged by MICHAEL STORY

GIMME SOME LOVIN'

Words and Music by
STEVE WINWOOD, MUFF WINWOOD
and SPENCER DAVIS
Arranged by MICHAEL STORY

Bright rock

HEDWIG'S THEME
(From "Harry Potter and the Sorcerer's Stone")

By JOHN WILLIAMS
Arranged by MICHAEL STORY

Mysteriously

PAINT IT BLACK

Words and Music by
MICK JAGGER and KEITH RICHARDS
Arranged by MICHAEL STORY

(I Can't Get No)
SATISFACTION

Words and Music by
MICK JAGGER and **KEITH RICHARDS**
Arranged by MICHAEL STORY

Bright rock

DON'T STOP BELIEVIN'

Words and Music by
JONATHAN CAIN, NEAL SCHON and STEVE PERRY
Arranged by MICHAEL STORY

16

Moderate rock

JAMES BOND THEME

By MONTY NORMAN
Arranged by MICHAEL STORY

MY IMMORTAL

Words and Music by
BEN MOODY, AMY LEE and DAVID HODGES
Arranged by MICHAEL STORY

* This bowing may be challenging to start with, but will make it easier once you master the style.

* If playing the cue notes, start with the up bow instead of the down bow.

THEME FROM "ICE CASTLES"
(Through the Eyes of Love)

Music by
MARVIN HAMLISCH
Arranged by MICHAEL STORY

D.C. al Coda

Coda

BLAZING SADDLES

By
MEL BROOKS and **JOHN MORRIS**
Arranged by **MICHAEL STORY**